Second Edition

Complete Beginner's
Woodcarving Workbook

A Simplified Approach for Learning to Carve

Mary Duke Guldan

FOX CHAPEL
PUBLISHING

ISBN 978-1-56523-745-2

Library of Congress Cataloging-in-Publication Data

Guldan, Mary Duke.
 Complete beginner's woodcarving workbook / Mary Duke Guldan.
    p. cm.
 Previously published: 2003
 ISBN 978-1-56523-745-2
 1. Wood-carving. 2. Wood-carving--Patterns. I. Title.
 TT199.7.G8396 2012
 736'.4--dc23
                    2012016328

To learn more about the other great books from Fox Chapel Publishing, or to find a retailer near you,
call toll-free 800-457-9112 or visit us at *www.FoxChapelPublishing.com*.

Note to Authors: We are always looking for talented authors to write new books. Please send a brief letter
describing your idea to Acquisition Editor, 1970 Broad Street, East Petersburg, PA 17520.

Printed in United States of America

First printing

Contents

To Peter and Ann
(my first students),
Aunt Katherine and
all those (of any age) who
are interested in learning...

Geophysical

Sun-Moon Clockface: Getting Started

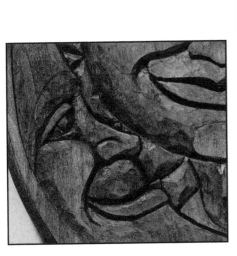

Sun and Moon Clock. This simple yet attractive piece can be carved using basic knives. This closeup shows how clean knife cuts define your project.

Sun-Moon Clockface, 14 inches tall x 12 inches wide, basswood carved in relief stained with artist's oil paint (burnt umber) mixed with Minwax Wipe-On Poly, a penetrating oil-based resin finish. The battery operated quartz clock movement is fully functional.

Sun-Moon Clockface

To learn to do wood carving, you will need a piece of wood and tools that will cut it. A scrap of wood leftover from a construction project will do, but it is more encouraging to start with a shaped plaque which has a nice finished edge. Check stores where craft or art supplies are sold. They may have a variety of pine and basswood plaques with router-trimmed edges. These are intended for painting and woodburning, but they are also good to carve.

If you have a choice, basswood is preferable because its grain is easier to work, and takes stain or paint very well. It is usually quite pale, nearly white, without obvious stripes of grain showing. It may feel slightly velvety to the touch, rather than slick and hard.

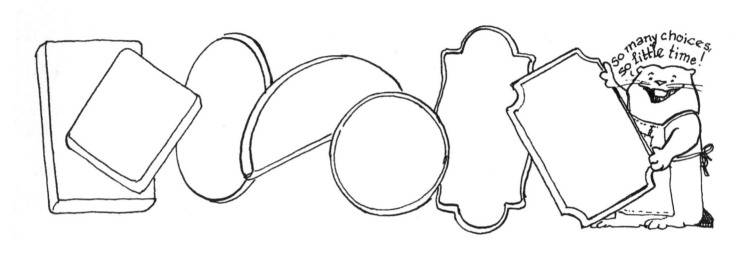

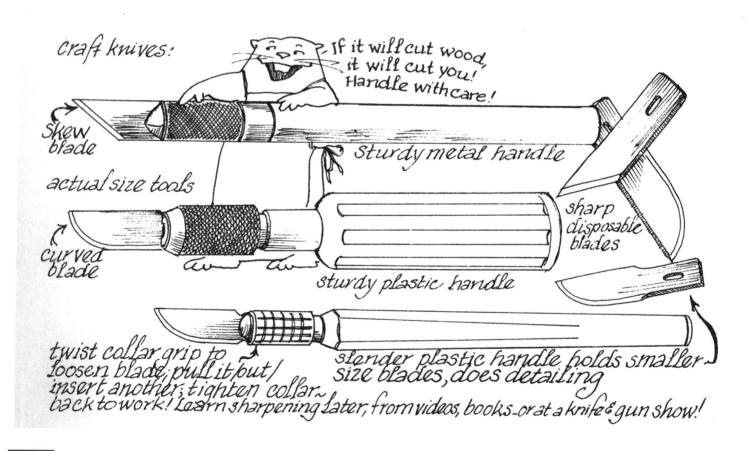

craft knives:

If it will cut wood, it will cut you! Handle with care!

Skew blade

Sturdy metal handle

actual size tools

sharp disposable blades

curved blade

sturdy plastic handle

twist collar grip to loosen blade; pull it out, insert another; tighten collar~ back to work! Learn sharpening later, from videos, books~or at a knife & gun show!

slender plastic handle holds smaller size blades, does detailing

X-Acto™ knives with interchangeable, disposable blade are great tools and are not a major investment. If you decide later that this skill is not for you, X-Acto™ knives can go to work in a wide variety of other applications.

You will need two kinds of blades: one with a slanted sharp edge and triangular point, the other with a curved sharp point. It is very helpful, especially was you get more involved, to have at least two handles: a large-diameter handle for heavier work, and a smaller one for detailing.

Grain: a big deal in carving

This little freckle is a knot, former base of a twig or branch that may have died & dropped off. The tree grew over the site, causing wrinkles in the grain to be avoided when you carve.

Grain

Grain!

across the grain

end grain } the openings of the sap tubes (don't cut as smoothly)

When you've gotten the wood and the tools, find the direction of the wood grain before you transfer the design to the piece. Grain is the striped pattern in lumber caused by the lengthwise cell walls of the tubes that carried moisture and nutrients through the trunk.

Using the curved blade, make a shallow scooping cut about an inch long, parallel to the grain lines up one edge of your lumber, or in the middle of the back of your plaque. Turn the wood around so that you can make the same cut going in the opposite direction. Compare the cuts: The one going with the grain felt smooth; the shaving came out cleanly with cupped ends. When you cut against the grain, you felt some splintery resistance; the chip has little ragged fibers on the end and preferred to crumble, rather than curl.

Basswood shows these characteristics less than most other kinds of wood, so is often used for carving.

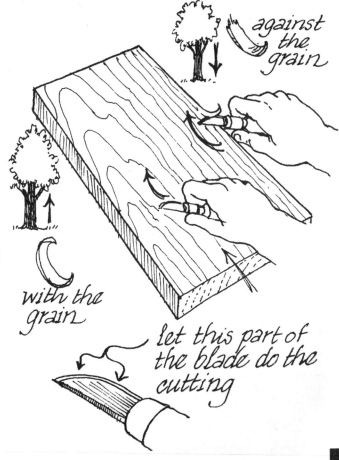

against the grain

with the grain

let this part of the blade do the cutting

This is your pattern~ it can be enlarged or reduced, if needed, to better fit your choice of wood. (An office photocopier can do this easily.) You can even trace just the moon, or the sun alone~turn the missing section of rays to the other side & trace those twice.

Grain lines should run vertically through most projects. The pattern should be placed so that it goes with the grain from its bottom toward its top, such as from chin to crown in a head or from foot to head in a full figure.

Now you'll need to trace or photocopy the pattern so it can be transferred to the wood. A quick substitute for carbon or transfer paper is to blacken the reverse side of your image with a soft-lead pencil. Lay the blackened side against the wood, tape it in place for security and draw firmly over the image with a ball point pen. The pencil lead on the back of your image will be imprinted on the wood.

Small works to be carved with knives can be held in your lap, resting on a sturdy board with a non-skid surface. I use a lap desk, a felt-covered piece of plywood 10 x 12 inches, with a small cushion attached on the back to make it self-leveling. It was meant for portable letter-writing and replaces a board wrapped in a retired bathtowel fastened on with safety pins.

sneak preview

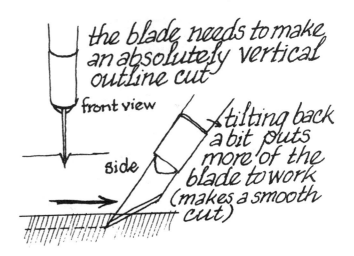

press & guide

pull

learning two-handed technique graduates to gouges & chisels later

Hold and power your knife with your dominant hand in a pencil-like position. Use your index finger of the opposite hand to add traction and direction. The blade should enter the wood vertically on this procedure. The minute it does you're no longer a complete beginner—you've begun!

There are all sorts of ways to hold the tools, but try this two-handed technique because it will exercise the two-handed powering and steering skills you'll need to use when you "graduate" to gouges and chisels.

the blade needs to make an absolutely vertical outline cut

front view

side

tilting back a bit puts more of the blade to work (makes a smooth cut)

Pull along the line about 3 inches,

then turn the work and continue

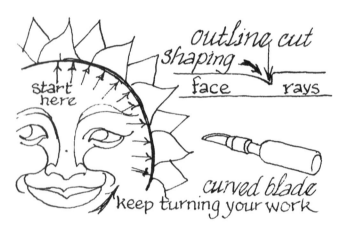

start here

outline cut

shaping

face   rays

curved blade

keep turning your work

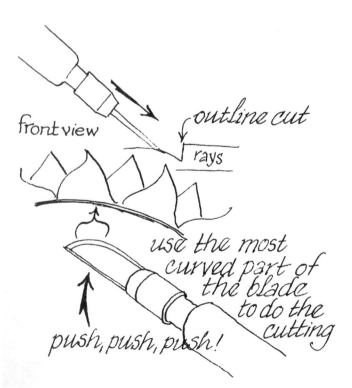

front view

outline cut

rays

use the most curved part of the blade to do the cutting

push, push, push!

Ready? Let's carve! Start on the circular outline of the sun's face with your skew knife (that's the one with the triangular point). Turn the sun sideways so you have the best access to the center of the top, and so you will be circling to the right, nearest yourself.

Pull the blade in a smooth effort, but not too fast for about three inches. Depth is not as important as accuracy. You can go back and recut, as many passes as are needed, following the trail you've already blazed, until the outline cut is about an eighth of an inch deep.

Turn your work and continue this outline cut another three inches, repeating the turning and cutting until you reach the chin. That's enough outlining for now!

Turn the sun right side up again, and begin shaping the edge of the face with the curved blade. Start your cuts about a fourth of an inch from the outline cut you just made. Push the most curved part of the blade into the wood at an angle that aims it at the bottom of your outline cut.

Go nipping along, turning the work as you go, so that you are always pushing the blade toward the outline.

If chips do not pop out, leaving a tidy trench, or if you find that the trench is not deep enough to make a shadow, recut your outline with the skew knife. Repeat the shaping cuts as needed. Stop just before you get to the chin oval.

Return to the top and make another pass, starting the shaping cuts farther from the outline, enlarging the curve at the edge of the face.

If your fingertips being to complain about the hard wear, prevent blisters by wrapping a Band-Aid around the offended area like a protective thimble.

The browline probably got carved off; take your pencil and draw it back. Now that you've had a little practice on this wood, let's have some fun with the features! Don't shriek in alarm, but get your skew knife and cut a firm outline form the brow intersection down the side of the nose. Start on the same side as your dominant hand. After the nose, cut the bottom browline.

With the curved blade and the same two-handed technique used to shape the face, cut a steep slope from the pencil browline into the bottom of the outline cut. Along the bridge of the nose, cut into the nose outline. Stop at the edge of the nostril for now, to reduce the chances of slipping and chipping.

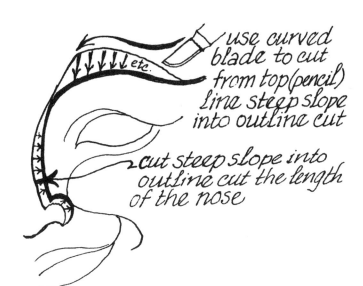

From the end of the pencil line that extends the eyelid, begin a gradual slope slanting into the outline. It curves all the way from the tip of the eyebrow down to the curve of the nose. Keep turning the project so that you can push smoothly into all these areas.

Hold the project up to see if these shapes are causing shadows that will make the image show. If the shadow is not strong enough, carve a deeper trench.

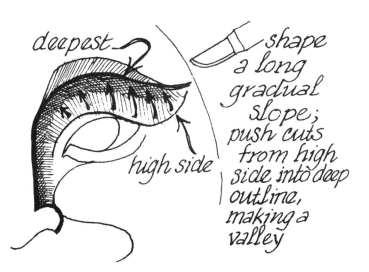

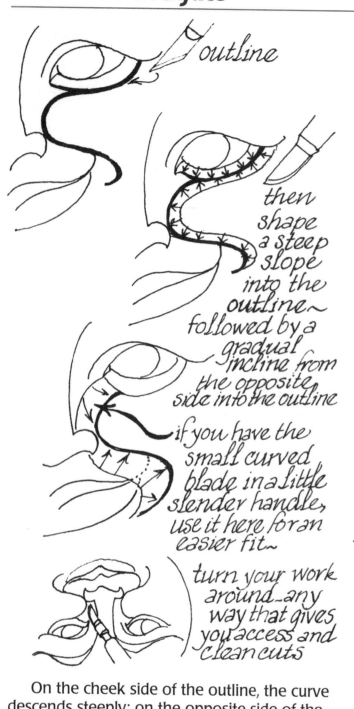

outline

then shape a steep slope into the outline~ followed by a gradual incline from the opposite side into the outline

if you have the small curved blade in a little slender handle, use it here for an easier fit~

turn your work around—any way that gives you access and clean cuts

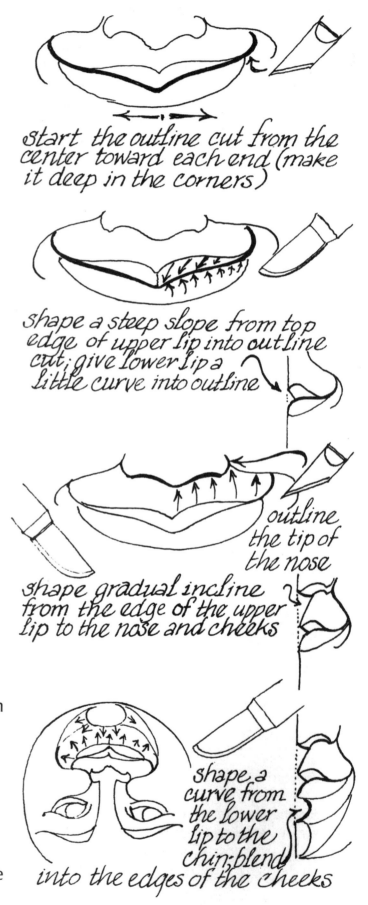

start the outline cut from the center toward each end (make it deep in the corners)

shape a steep slope from top edge of upper lip into outline cut; give lower lip a little curve into outline

outline the tip of the nose

shape gradual incline from the edge of the upper lip to the nose and cheeks

shape a curve from the lower lip to the chin; blend into the edges of the cheeks

On the cheek side of the outline, the curve descends steeply; on the opposite side of the outline, the curve begun over the eye and down beside the nose extends smoothly. As the curve continues past the edge of the nose, you'll lose your mouth corner. Pencil it back quickly.

Before you forget how you manage these areas, carve the corresponding brow, nose and check on the opposite side.

Note, as you do the mouth and chin, that the upper lip and chin get no outline cuts.

With your accumulated skills, let's do the eyes! Yes, they are the most critical features that really bring your carving to life. But before you panic, there are some excellent wood patching compounds now available, so that you can cover your mistakes, recarve and hide the difference in materials under a nice coat of paint.

Round the whole eye area with the curv-ed blade. Include the lids; recess the corners.

Take your pencil and redraw the lids. Scribe their outlines with the skew blade, paying special attention to the corners.

Use the skew blade to shave the eyeballs into plump spheres, so that they are stepped back from the eyelids. Clean out all stray chips and fibers, being again especially careful to cleat the corners. The skew blade is used to round the eyeballs because it leaves no trace of a concave dimple like the curved blade would, so it makes a smoother sphere.

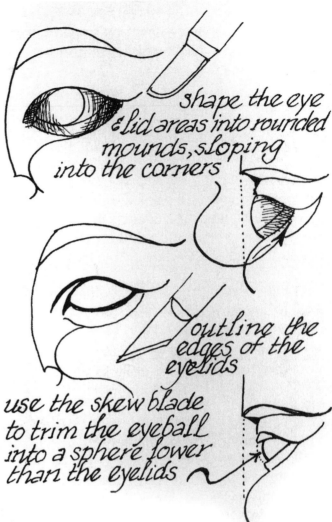

shape the eye & lid areas into rounded mounds, sloping into the corners

outline the edges of the eyelids

use the skew blade to trim the eyeball into a sphere lower than the eyelids

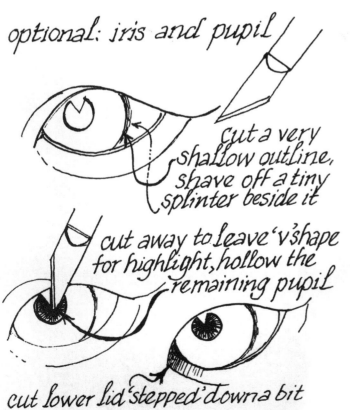

optional: iris and pupil

Cut a very shallow outline, shave off a tiny splinter beside it

cut away to leave 'v' shape for highlight, hollow the remaining pupil

cut lower lid 'stepped' down a bit

Here you'll need to decide if you'd rather paint, stain or carve the iris and pupils into the eyes.

These details can be done with the skew knife. Turn the knife with its point toward the center of the pupil, blade toward the outside, slicing a v-shaped highlight in each. No chip should come out.

Next carefully ream the remaining pupil space into a conical depression.

The edge of the iris, the colored part of the eye, is defined by a sliver. Cut a shallow outline; remove a thin shaving from outside it.

Wow, this is an engaging little face! It needs a buddy.

Sun-Moon Clockface

Put your "sun" skills to work here, and since the moon face involves a much smaller area, you may do so well, so quickly that you'll surprise yourself!

A sharp, clean outline is essential, especially along the profile adjoining the sun. Use the skew knife to cut very firmly into corners at the tips of the crescent, under the nose and along the mouth.

When shaping the edges of the moon with the curved blade, round them in several passes as you did the sun's edges.

Outline the features next, setting the skew point firmly into corners, especially when following the eye and lid line.

The slope from the brow to eyelid is slight, but the curve at the bulge of the cheek is steep and deep.

Blend the beginning of the brow into the bridge of the nose, dipping the curve below the level of the eyes. To keep the ray area out front from being so fragile, lower the level of the rays nearest the tip of the moon's nose.

Turn the whole upper lip into a rounded mound. Make the mouth a deep, but narrow trench.

Round the lower lip the same as you did the sun's, lowering the corner that tucks beneath the cheek. Trim from underneath the lip without outlining, so that it forms a curved shelf. Scoop a shallow depression from the cheeks to the elongated chin.

The eyelids are steeply slanted into the brow and cheek. Turn your skew knife sideways to get the eyeball rounded right into the corner.

The moon's eye should match the sun's detailing. If those were carved, you'll be relieved to see that the iris edge is a sliver and the pupil highlight a tiny triangular chip.

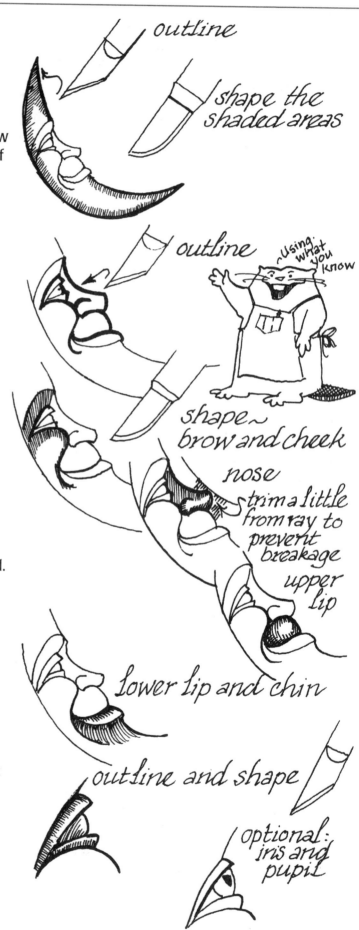

outline

shape the shaded areas

outline

~Using what you know

shape~ brow and cheek

nose

trim a little from ray to prevent breakage

upper lip

lower lip and chin

outline and shape

optional: iris and pupil

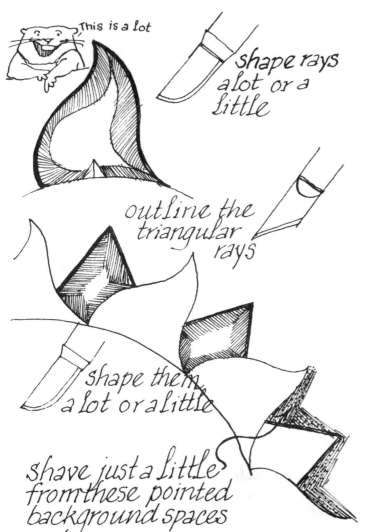

for clock faces, notch the numeral locations first~ outline four wavy rays; make firm cuts from points, both at outside ends and by the face

This is a lot

shape rays a lot or a little

outline the triangular rays

shape them a lot or a little

shave just a little from these pointed background spaces

Carving the rays will give you a chance to learn to work around grain direction. Eventually you will cross it, go against it, or may even come to an unpredictable irregularity.

Plaques made of boards glued side to get enough width may have grain going in opposite directions.

Turn your work in any direction that you need in order to make clean cuts. If the grain seems resistant to being carved from a direction, turn your work around and try the cut from another way.

If you plan to use this carving for a clock face, there is a little mark in the center of each wavy ray edge marking locations of the numerals. Make a little notch on each of these so that you'll know their places, regardless of the shaping.

(Plastic numerals with self-adhesive backs probably are sold where you purchased the clock movement.)

Starting at the top on the wavy rays, scribe the outlines of four with the skew knife. Shape them with your curved blade as little or as much as you like, then move on to do the next four.

When you reach the moon, the rays are somewhat hidden. With the exception of the ray by the bridge of the moon's nose, which will be kept like a little plateau because we need its shadow, make other rays seem to dip down behind the moon.

When all the wavy rays have been completed, outline the triangular rays with the skew knife, taking care to get crisp points on their tips. Shape them with the curved blade, especially where they dip behind the wavy rays.

Last shaping of all, trim a little from the pointed parts of the border, so the detailing on those rays will show in all its glory!

Sun-Moon Clockface

Wow, the carving's done! Before you paint or stain, you'll want to drill a hole for the clock movement.

Battery-operated quartz clock movements are available at craft supply stores, some hardware stores and by mail order. (This one came from the craft store where the plaque was purchased and cost about $5. They work remarkably well and are not complicated to install.) In making your selection, be certain that the shaft to which the hands will be fastened is long enough to go through you board. Package labeling will tell the clockface thickness there are shafts for dials like ours, three quarters of an inch (19mm) thick.

After you've drilled a suitable shaft here, you'll need to paint or stain your carving before you install the movement. Acrylic paints work well and allow you to paint in some terrific extra detailing. Stains are also effective.

As preciously mentioned, self-stick plastic numerals are available, which you might like to add when the finish dries. You could paint on your own numbers, if you'd rather.

The clock movements have a built-in hanger in the back of the case. There are additional hangers made to slip over the shaft, but I relocated the hanger nearer the top of the plaque. It is a little block of wood with a notch in its center, glued and screwed for added security.

When the movement has been installed and you've put in the battery, the rascal is off and running! So are you!

Installing the 'clockworks' (follow the manufacturer's directions)... usually, just drill a hole large enough for the clock shaft to fit through~

the movement is secured with a rubber gasket on the back and a hexnut on the front~press hands on the shaft in order, secured by a hexnut...

helps, of course, if you can tell time!

usually there is a little hanger built into the back of the case

there are heavy duty hangers made to slip over the shaft, but you can glue and screw a small notched block at the top...

Leaping Buck: Putting in a Background

Leaping Buck. This sign or plaque in relief can be carved using only basic knives. See the following pages to incorporate relief designs in furniture and other projects.

Leaping buck, 16½ inches long x 8½ inches tall, basswood
carved in relief, stained with artist's oil paint (Paynes gray) mixed with
Minwax Wipe-On Poly.

A closeup photo at an angle showing the depth of wood you are removing to create a relief effect.

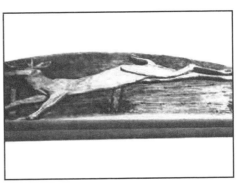

Overall project at an angle showing the profile of this piece.

This is your pattern—the dotted perspective lines on the top and bottom of the fence will help you add more posts of appropriate height if needed. Otherwise, don't transfer the dots to your project. This pattern can be reduced or enlarged.

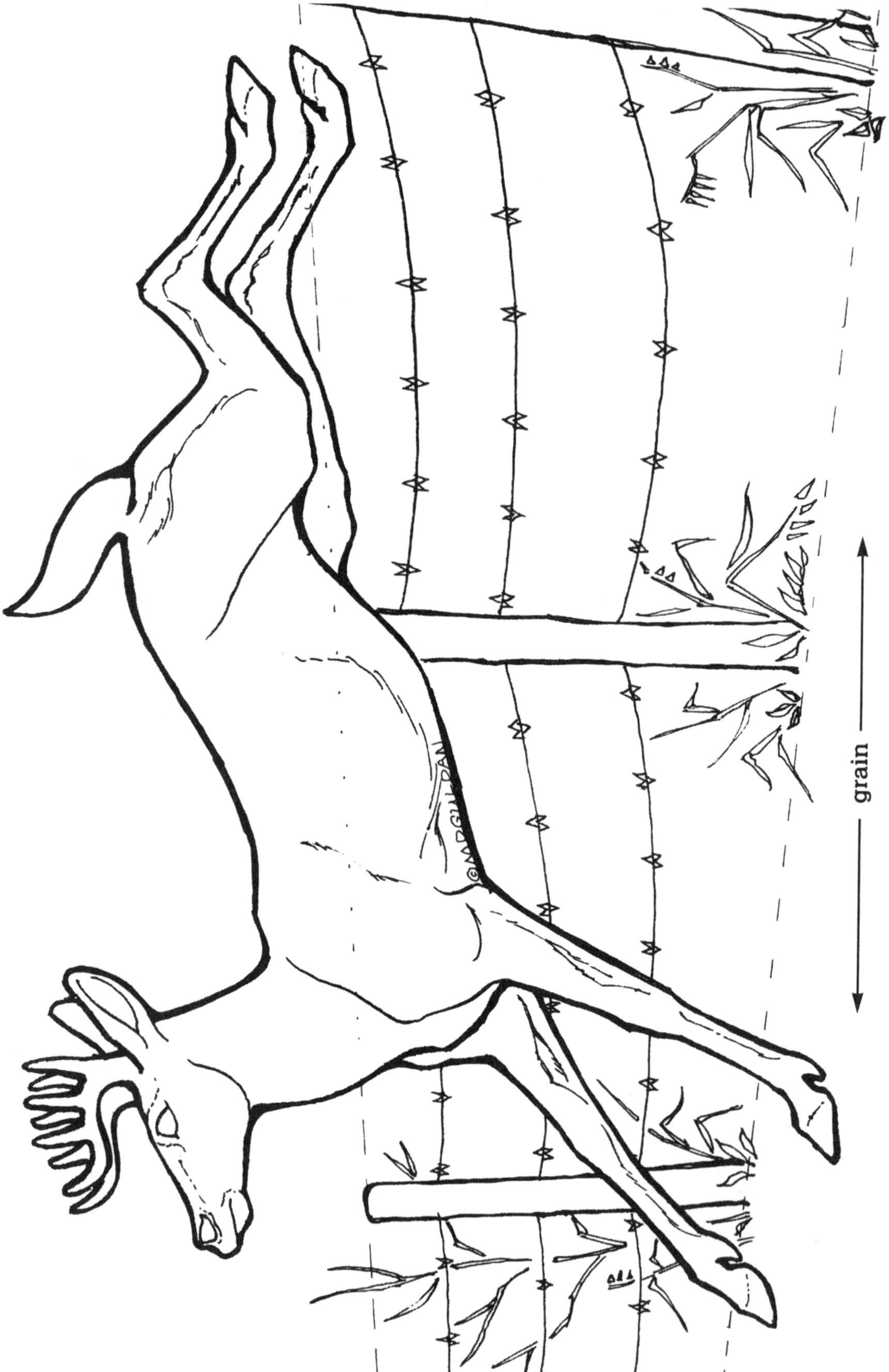

grain

©MARGUERITE DAN

There are lots of ways to use a nice relief!

Now that you've got a grip on your equipment, let's try a pictorial relied that can include scenery. This one is fun because you can do as much or as little carving on it as you like, and it will still be effective. If you like to paint, you'll have an excellent subject here.

Before you get this buck underway, give a thought to some of the ways you could use the finished project. That might make a difference when you shop for wood. Of course, it does make a popular decorative image as is, but it also can be a very handsome base for clothes hooks. I had a buck's rack with a badly splintered brow tine (there must have been a story there!) so I didn't mind sawing off the good antler and securing it to the bottom of a buck plaque. Hanging beside the back door, it's ideal for caps and hats.

A longer board with a straight edge along one side could be mounted over a door or window or above a gun over a mantle.

If you can just see the buck as a crown molding atop a gun cabinet or bookcase, shop for L-shaped shelf brackets in a hardware department. The ones intended to be bolted to the bottom of a board shelf and then to the wall can easily be reversed; screwed to the back of your carving and the top of the cabinet. When you decide to move either one, the screws can be removed to with minimal effect on either your carving or the furniture.

Similarly, to fasten the relief to the back of a bench or hunt board buffet, screw several wooden braces to the back of your work, with sufficient lengths extending below the carving to allow screws through the braces to secure it to the back of the furniture.

With all of these possibilities, plus the ones you think up yourself, your biggest challenge is going to be choosing just one destination for your carving!

Leaping Buck

You've selected the wood to fit your intentions and have the pattern ready. Now transfer just the outline of the deer to the wood. With your skew knife outline him firmly, taking special care to cut cleanly into corners.

skip this for now

outline starting here

With the curved blade, start with little nibbles, clearing a trench of varying width around the figure. Keep turning your work so that you can push the blade into the outline, using a two-hand assisted cut. Around the main part of the body, this outline trench should be about a fourth of an inch deep, less around the extremities.

If you like, you may stop carving when you've got a well-defined outline. In that case, skip over to the detailing of hooves, antlers and features.

Such a buck could have detailing and scenery painted in, if you like.

vary the width of your shading cuts for descriptive shadows

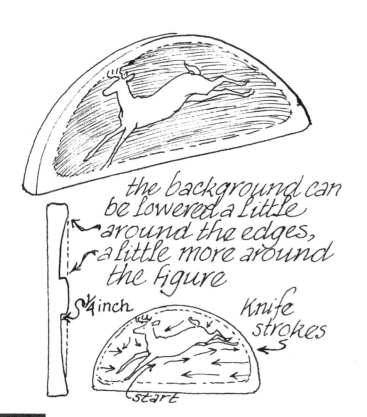

the background can be lowered a little around the edges, a little more around the figure

¼ inch

Knife strokes

start

If on the other hand, you like snipping out little chips, here's your chance to make enough chips to keep a hamster happy for weeks! Texture the background with a multitude of little cuts, very shallow around the outside edge, going deeper in the center.

A small curved blade in a slender handle works very well here. Start by the buck's body cutting a slope to widen the outline trench. Gradually widen the graded area until it slopes up and out to the perimeter where the cuts barely dimple the surface. This does not have to be particularly even or leveled because the background is going to be broken up by the scenery.

Back to the buck. Outline the chest and overlapped edge of the hind leg with your skew blade. With the curved blade, flake off a thin layer from the background legs, from joint to body so that these will be on a lower level than the foreground legs.

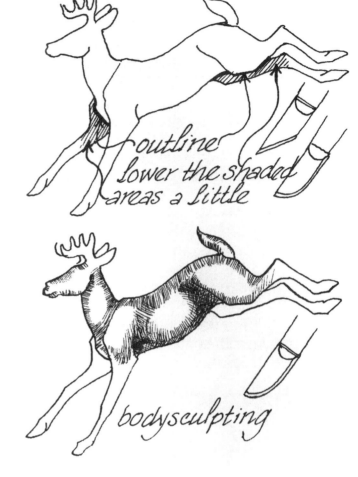

Shaping the body mainly involves rounding its contours into the outline cut. The shaded areas show where the shaping can be wider and more elaborate. On the shoulder and hip use the outline-less technique you premiered on the sun's chin. You did not scribe an outline, you began shaving a curve ahead of the contour.

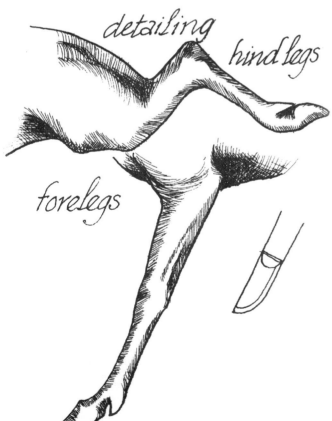

Detailing the legs is more of the same techniques: rounding the outlines a good bit, or very little. Taking a triangular chip of the back of the ankle will define the dewclaws. To show the tendons on the backs of the lower legs, as well as the muscles in the forearms and rump, cut a series of shallow strokes to form half the depression from the right side. Cut a second series from the left, meeting the first in the middle.

Even though deer hooves are cloven, do not bother trying to include the split between them when seen from this angle.

Leaping Buck

The detailing continues. With the skew knife, outline the mouth, eye, near antler and ear. Remove a sliver from the lower lip, cut out a triangular chip to clear the nostril. Round the eyeball. Shave a hollow inside the ear. The skew blade can also be used to clear between the antler tines.

Use the curved knife to clear the rest of the background without digging little nicks. Pencil in the location of the other ear and antler and lower their background slightly. Round the antler's edges the least little bit.

You can stop now, and will have a very handsome image, but the background can be impressive, and fun besides!

Pencil in fence posts; use the dotted lines on the pattern to help get the perspective if your wood needs more fence. They are not

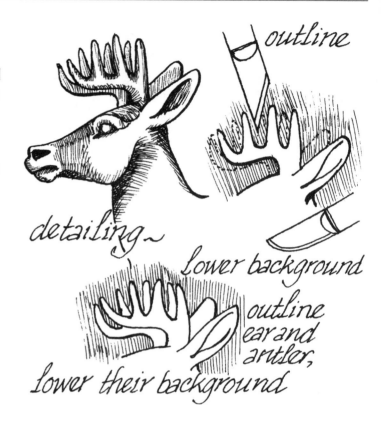

detailing ~ outline lower background outline ear and antler, lower their background

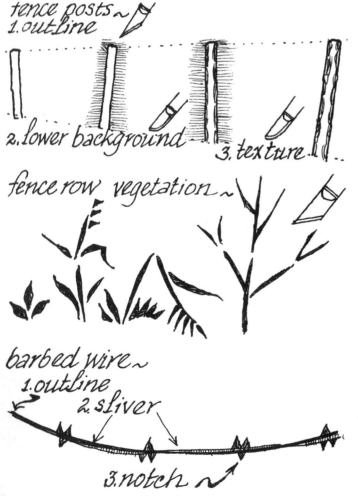

fence posts ~
1. outline
2. lower background
3. texture

fence row vegetation ~

barbed wire ~
1. outline
2. sliver
3. notch

too vertical, not too smooth, and smaller in the distance. Scribe their outlines with the skew blade. Use the curved blade to shave a slightly lower background right around them. A few uneven strokes up each side will give them a weathered wood texture.

Pencil in clumps of overgrown grass, weeds and a sapling, then the sagging strands of wire.

To carve the weeds, cut out little slivers for the rugged texture, a stroke from each side. Make these little trenches vary in width, as well as shape.

This image is about a buck, not the fence, so we're doing it in a very sketchy style. Scribe each row of wire in a firm outline stroke. Shave skinny slivers from alternate sides of the outline to make the twisted strands. Although in reality, there are four barbs per cluster, carve just three tiny triangular chips. On the distant wires, make the barbs smaller and closer together.

Now, paint or stain to suit yourself!

Dog Figures: Working in Three Dimensions

These dogs make a perfect beginner's whittling project.

Dogs, 3 inches tall x 4 inches long, and 2 inches tall x 2 1/8 inches long, carved from a lumber cut-out, stained with artist's oil paints (burnt umber and Paynes gray). A larger scale dog figure can be carved using the dog from the Faithful Dog pattern.

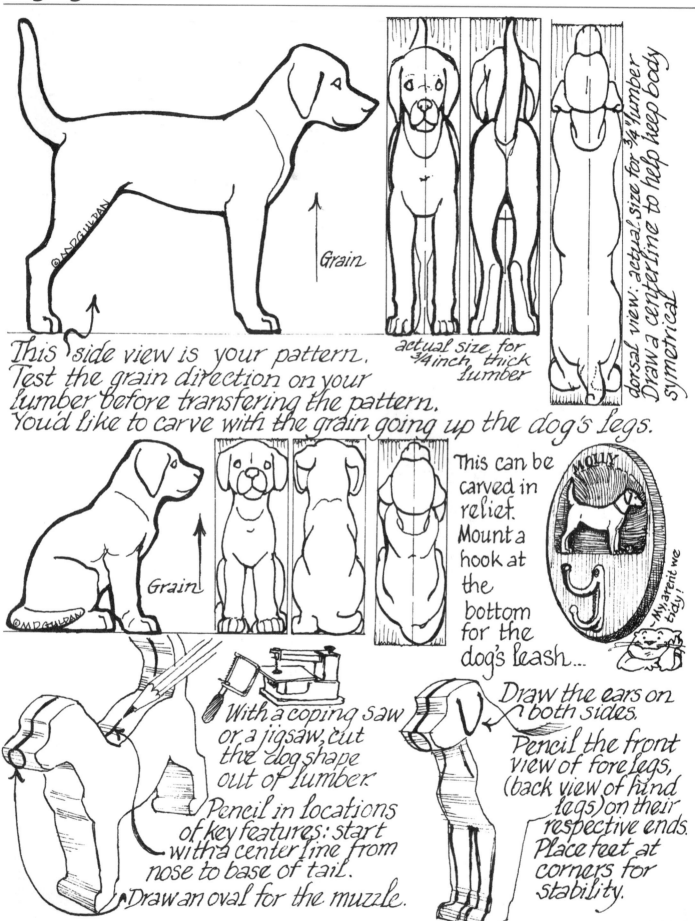

Grain

actual size for ¾ inch thick lumber

dorsal view: actual size for ¾" lumber. Draw a centerline to help keep body symetrical

This side view is your pattern. Test the grain direction on your lumber before transfering the pattern. You'd like to carve with the grain going up the dog's legs.

Grain

This can be carved in relief. Mount a hook at the bottom for the dog's leash...

MOLLY

~ My, aren't we tidy!

With a coping saw or a jigsaw, cut the dog shape out of lumber.

Pencil in locations of key features: start with a center line from nose to base of tail.

Draw an oval for the muzzle.

Draw the ears on both sides.

Pencil the front view of fore legs, (back view of hind legs) on their respective ends. Place feet at corners for stability.

Rather than seizing your curved knife in your fist and pulling with your whole arm, try this technique utilizing the natural strength of your grasp. Brace your dominant thumb on the front of the work, push toward the knuckles, "feeding" the wood into the blade. At the same time, the fingers of that hand pull the blade forward powered by curling your hand. Snip small curved chips in a series of little scooping cuts.

Your other hand steadies the work from underneath on the opposite side. Bracing the work and your hands on your lap board is helpful.

try curling your hand to power the blade

Now that you know the technique, let's put it to work on the dog. Cut a small amount from each side of the tail to make it less cumbersome. Work from the tip toward the dock, but save enough to wag.

The hips will be more accessible now, so start rounding edges from rump to neck; first on one side, then the other. This will take several passes, rounding a bit more each time.

Between the shoulders and the ears, the neck is kind of narrow, so your rounding efforts can extend down the sides of the neck. The ears' outline cuts should cause the chips from the neck to pop right off, leaving the ears sticking up like tiny cliffs.

Check the dorsal view diagram to see the dog's body from overhead; note where the body widens and narrows. Now look at the shaded side view here, and start at the heels, shaping the sides of the dog's body. Darker shaded areas indicate where more wood needs to be removed.

Work first on one side, then on the other to keep the body balance.

outline both ears

trim a little from each side of the tail, then work forward

Looks like a case of 'man bites dog'

turn the work for best access

Dog Figures

Trim from the side of the dog's face toward the muzzle so the head narrows to the size of your penciled oval. Round the edges, especially over the bridge of the nose. The curve over the top of the skull begins at the "roots" of the ears. Slant the ears from back toward the front.

If you can manage this small snip of authenticity, there is a tiny dip above the bridge of the nose, right between the eyes.

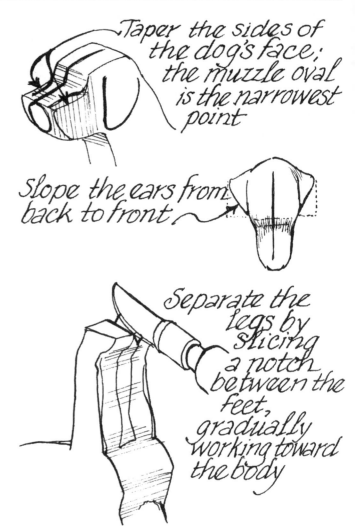

Taper the sides of the dog's face; the muzzle oval is the narrowest point

Slope the ears from back to front.

Front and hind legs are both separated the same way: Start from the outside, slice a notch between the feet. From the front of the forelegs and back of the hind, cut a narrow trench the length of the proposed opening. Make repeated passes from the feet toward the body, slicing deeper v-shaped cuts until you finally cut all the way through.

Separate the legs by slicing a notch between the feet, gradually working toward the body

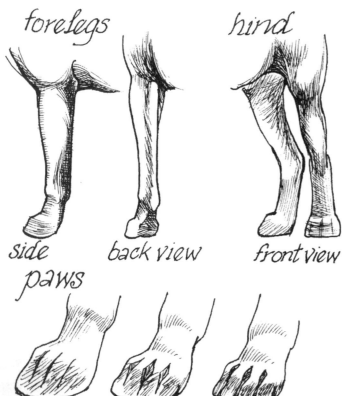

forelegs   hind

side   back view   front view

paws

Once you know the contour of the opening, you can slice a bit from its opposite side to help with the clearing. Use the point of the skew knife to open the chest area.

When the opening has been made, shape the legs; rounded over the muscles in front, narrow over the tendons up the back. Give the forelegs elbow peaks; hollow little depressions in the ribcage behind them. Round the edges of the belly; cut a little hollow in the flank just ahead of each hind leg. The belly ends in a very tight v between the hind legs.

Trim the paws; rounded across the front with sloping toes, like little horse hooves. Pencil the locations of four toes a piece. At the edge of the knuckles, cut a tiny notch for each, cutting a matching sliver from the bottom edge of each toe.

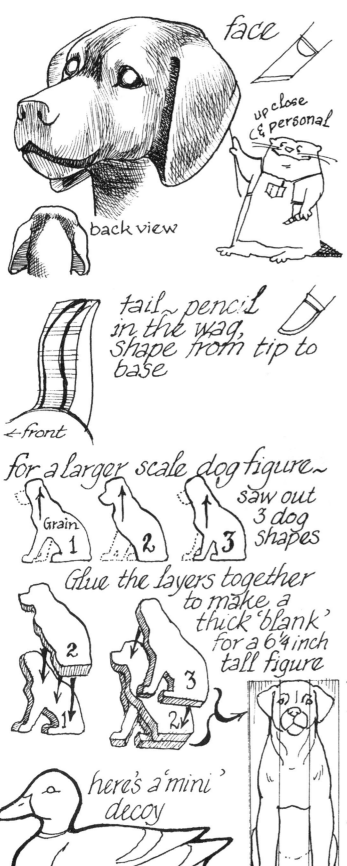

face

up close & personal

back view

tail~ pencil in the wag, Shape from tip to base

←front

for a larger scale dog figure~

saw out 3 dog shapes

Grain 1   2   3

Glue the layers together to make a thick 'blank' for a 6¼ inch tall figure

2   3   1   2

here's a 'mini' decoy

1cm.=1in.scale

The pattern can be adapted to a Labrador Retriever...

actual size

Plan facial features in pencil first, and then scribe their outlines with the point of the skew knife. Remove tiny chips to form the features. The cuts to define the outlines of the ears can slant inward a little. Nip a little chip from under the bottom of the ear without getting it too thin, then you can round under the jaw and neck.

Pencil the maximum wag in the available tail space. Carve from tip to base until you reach your pencil line, rounding it carefully afterward.

Now, you're ready to paint or stain—or flee from your success, since your viewers all want you to make dogs for them!

The same techniques and procedure will work in other scales. You can carve the puppy in the same way, and will be glad to note that his little tail is most conveniently curled around his hind legs.

For a larger scale dog, use the pattern from the next project. If you'd like to turn the Rottweiler into a Labrador Retriever, substitute the head below. To that project you might like to add a few mini decoys.

Instead of carving a relief, saw out the dog shape from lumber and glue together a stack of three layers to get enough thickness for a dog that size.

Squeeze the layers between a clamp or two to get a good glue bond and let it dry overnight before you carve.

Faithful Dog:
Learning to Use Gouges and Chisels

Faithful Dog *carved in relief combines the use of knives and gouges.*

Closeup photo at an angle showing the profile of Faithful Dog *in relief.*

Faithful Dog, 10½ inches tall x 8½ inches, basswood plaque, carved in relief using all the tools in a beginner's basic boxed set, stained with artist's oil paint (Paynes gray) mixed with Minwax Wipe-On Poly.

To make this pattern fit your wood, make the 'tree' border taller, and add bricks to make the wall wider, as needed.

Faithful Dog

If you've enjoyed carving with craft knives, you might want to advance to gouges and chisels. We'll exercise a new set of skills on another relief. This one will give you opportunities to try the different shapes of tools that some in a basic boxed set, ideal for beginners. Check an art of craft supply store, or where woodworking tools are sold, though these can be purchased by mail order if you don't find them for sale locally. They cost around $35 for a set of the six most basic shapes; they come with handles on, sharpened and ready to use. Make no mistake; these are not toys but are good tools. With proper maintenance, they will last your lifetime and will still be just as functional for detailing when you've moved up to carving ships' figureheads, cigar store Indians and full-sized carousel horses!

Carving tools can be push-powered, but tapping with a woodcarver's mallet powers the blade through routine wood removal when you begin shaping. It offers great control; when the taps stop, the blade stops. Slips and gashes are usually avoided. Mallet heads are tapered cylinders, so that anywhere they strike is a good place, quite unlike targeting the small head on a claw hammer. If you have a choice, your first mallet should be small and lightweight for these smaller pieces.

The work needs to be fastened down to keep it from moving, which would be dangerous for you and your project. Clamp the work to the edge of a sturdy table or countertop. Pieces of an old leather belt can be cut to pad the clamp jaws, preventing scars on the work or the work place.

Working around the clamp will seem a little cumbersome at first, because you want to avoid hitting it and breaking a blade. You will soon get used to each other! These are two-handed tools, not to be used in your lap, knife style. Just wait 'til you see what they can do!

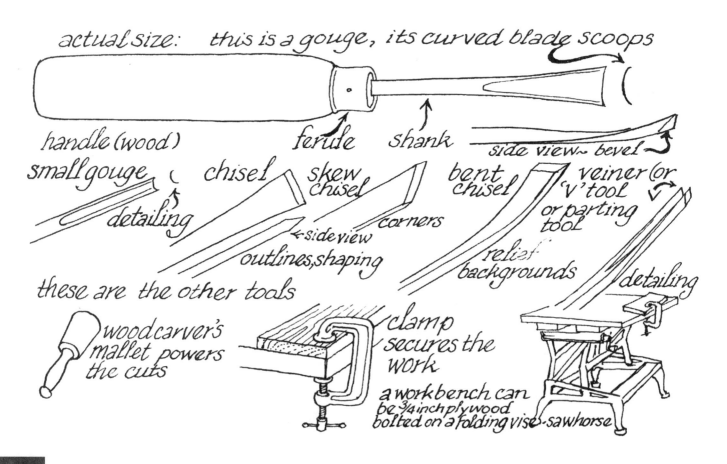

actual size: this is a gouge, its curved blade scoops

handle (wood)   ferule   shank   side view~ bevel

small gouge   chisel   skew chisel   bent chisel   veiner (or 'v' tool or parting tool)

detailing   ←side view   outlines, shaping   corners   relief backgrounds   detailing

these are the other tools

woodcarver's mallet powers the cuts

clamp secures the work

a workbench can be ¾ inch plywood bolted on a folding vise-sawhorse

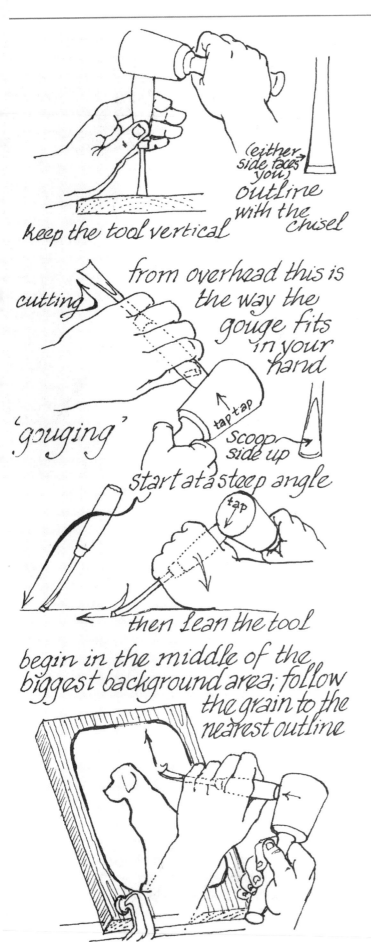

keep the tool vertical

(either side faces you)

outline with the chisel

cutting

from overhead this is the way the gouge fits in your hand

'gouging'

tap tap

scoop side up

start at a steep angle

tap

then lean the tool

begin in the middle of the biggest background area; follow the grain to the nearest outline

Transfer only the image of the dog and outline of the border to the wood. Clamp it securely by a bottom corner. With your chisel and mallet, outline the tree trunk border. Operate the mallet with you dominant hand because it already knows the hammering routine. Don't clench your other fist around the chisel or you'll absorb all the mallet's power.

Steady your wrist on the work, pinch the tool between your thumb and fingers enough to hold it vertical. Tap, tap, tap (not pound!) it with the mallet until it sinks bevel deep into the wood. No chip should come out during this procedure. Free the tool by gently rocking left/right, set it next to the first cut so that its corner barely overhangs that little slot, ensuring no missed fibers that might splinter later. Tap, tap, tap again. You'd like to cut about an eighth of an inch deep.

When you have inched around the border, outline the outside of the dog.

Now you're ready to use the gouge and make lots of chips! Get out in the open in the background, going with the grain toward the outline. Hold the gouge with your fingers curled around it, braced by the pad of your thumb tip. Don't clench your fist tightly here, either. Hold the blade up at a steeper angle for the first couple of mallet taps to make the bevel bite into the wood, scoop side up. Keep tapping as you rock the tool back so that its bevel is parallel to the board. Tap, tap, tap— the chip curls up on top of your blade as you carve along! This feels like real carving! The chip should pop out as soon as you reach the outline cut. Oh wow, your first!

If it does not, remove the gouge while you take the chisel and cut the outline a little deeper. If your gouge gets stuck, free it as you would the chisel, by rocking gently left/right, from side to side.

Faithful Dog

Chip by chip in side by side cuts, clear as much of your background as you can reach. The gouge leaves a slightly ridged surface, but try to keep the depth as level as possible. Change the clamp location, repositioning your work so that the entire background can be cleared. You'll notice that carving against the grain is a big issue with these tools. Change direction, doing little test chips until you get clean cut. Keep the ridges parallel.

There's a small area of background between the dog's legs and body; now that you've had a chance to use your tools, cautiously outline and clear this confined area.

Next, take your bent chisel and try it gently, hand-powered, smoothing a few high ridges in the background to see how it behaves. The whole background could be made quite smooth, but let's save some of the gouge texture. Instead, smooth the areas that will be the gate posts, and a small margin around the border and the dog.

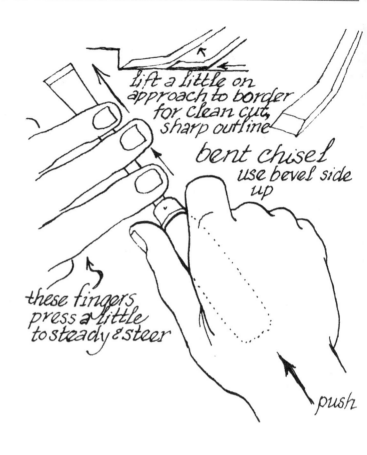

lift a little on approach to border for clean cut, sharp outline

bent chisel use bevel side up

these fingers press a little to steady & steer

push

Pencil in the gate posts, widening or narrowing them to fit your plaque. Using your veiner, cut all of the straight parts of the gate, starting with the horizontal bars, turning them into little trenches. Keep the cuts the same depth as the veiner's bevels. Avoid rocking the tools as you cut or it will grab more of one side than the other.

Above the scrolled ornament there is a sturdy frame across the gate top. Cut this with the veiner, from each side, meeting in the middle.

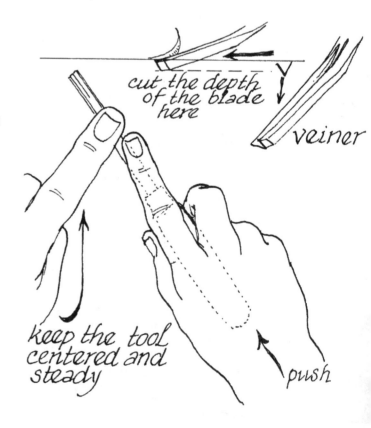

cut the depth of the blade here

veiner

keep the tool centered and steady

push

Take a break of sorts, and shape the dog; since you've just worked on dog anatomy, use your craft knives if you like. The large gouge is fun to use in modeling round the shoulders, flanks and hips.

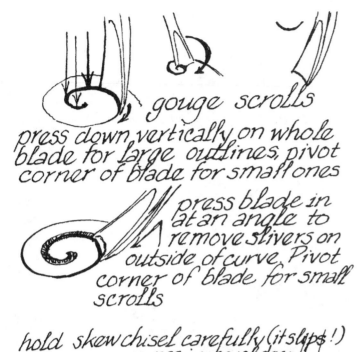

gouge scrolls

press down vertically on whole blade for large outlines, pivot corner of blade for small ones

press blade in at an angle to remove slivers on outside of curve. Pivot corner of blade for small scrolls

hold skew chisel carefully (it slips!) press in bevel-deep to outline 'arrows'

skew chisel

reverse blade, tilt slightly toward arrow center

small gouge cuts mortar joints

use skew chisel to cut triangular chips for erosion (stagger or alternate joints for realism)

Let's get back to the gate detailing by doing the scrolls. These can be carved with the skew craft knife, but try this with your large gouge instead. It can be used to carve different sized of scrolls, depending on the amount of blade you use. Start on a large scroll, in its center, outlining, by pressing vertically, at least bevel deep. For a tight turn, use just a corner of the blade.

When the outline has been cut, make a second pass. This time, press the blade into the outline at an oblique angle, making a little trench. Snip these little slivers from the outside of the curve. On a small scroll, try a careful pivot using the corner of the blade.

For a little bead at the center of the spiral, use your small gouge and do two tiny scoops which meet in the center.

Use your skew chisel to cut the decorative arrows. Be careful, it will easily slip and gash on its slanted bevel. Press the tip deeper than the heel to outline the arrow. Turn the blade over, point down, bevel out in front like a miniature plow. Tilt it slightly toward the arrow's center, push to the point. After the corresponding cut on the arrow's other side, a v-shaped chip should pop out. The skew chisel is an excellent chip-snipper.

Outline the bricks with the small gouge, horizontal mortar joints first. Stagger the vertical joints, and use the skew chisel to nip out triangular chips to show weathering.

Texture the ground with shallow horizontal strokes of the small gouge. This makes an inconspicuous surface that could be a path, a lawn or paved walk.

Light large gouge strokes on the borders put bark on the trees. Cut the little tree branches with your gouges not nearly as deep as the other background, suggesting a wooden avenue. And now, you are ready to paint or stain!

Cherubs: Carving Faces

Angels and Cherubs.

Cherubs, 6 inches long x 3 inches high, sawed outlines with stacked layer for extra depth on full-face version, stained with artist's oil pants (burnt umber).

this is a single layer of ¾ inch thick lumber and can be done with craft knives

this is two layers of wood glued together (to be carved with gouges & chisels)

1.

Layer 1 ~ wings & head

(2) ↑ Grain

Layer 2 ~ head only

Glue 2 on top of 1 for extra dimension in the face

clamp the layers until the glue dries for a good bond (pad the clamp jaws to prevent 'bruising' the wood ~ use pieces cut from an old smooth leather belt)

Layer 1

Layer 2

Cherubs

Once you've worked with the purposeful cuts those gouges and chisels deliver, you'll start looking around for other ways to use them! These cherub heads are a modern nod to an old Bavarian custom of handing one above a child's bed as a reminder of his guardian angel watching over him. As a toddler, I climbed atop my sister's crib rails so that I could reach up and feel the face and wings of the nearest angel. The full face view is based on it, though this subject has long been a popular decorative motif.

These projects can be carved as a regular relied in the center of a plaque, but sawing the shape out of lumber will give them the illusion of greater depth.

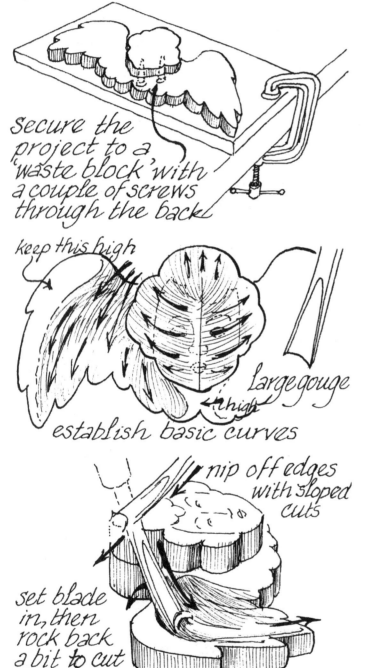

Secure the project to a 'waste block' with a couple of screws through the back

keep this high

establish basic curves

Large gouge

high

nip off edges with sloped cuts

set blade in, then rock back a bit to cut scooped out hollow

Since you have by now had a lot of practice doing a relief on a single thickness of wood, let's concentrate on the full-face, done with gouges and chisels. For shaping on a small and detailed piece, fasten the work to a "waste black" so that your clamp will not be in your way and your work area is protected from stray cuts. A piece of quarter inch thick plywood is splintery but tough and can be reused indefinitely. Run screws through the plywood into the back of the work where it's thickest.

Use mallet power and your large gouge. Start rounding the top of the head by snipping off its edge in a series of cuts begun about half an inch from the "cliff." Work down each side of the face, leaving just the chin intact. On subsequent passes, begin the curve nearer the center until only a centerline where the nose will be and the chin are unaffected.

The wings need to have a slightly scooped hollow in the center. After tapping the gouge at a steep angle to begin each cut, rock it back on its bevel to get it to scoop. Depending on the character of your wood, you may need to cut from the top and from the bottom, meeting in the middle. Don't let the wing edges get too thin.

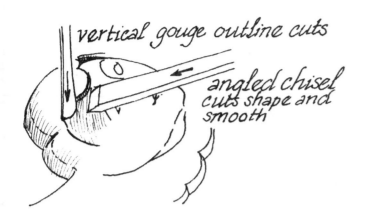

vertical gouge outline cuts

angled chisel cuts shape and smooth

Pencil in the hairline and features on the newly rounded head. Make the outline cuts for the hairline around the forehead between the brows and hairline. The hairline will become raised like a little ledge.

Use the large gouge to hollow the eye sockets just a little. Begin at the center beside the nose; making little cupped scoops, follow the curve of the eyebrow. Clean up stray fibers on the cheek side.

gouge gently shallow eye sockets

Redraw the eyes and outline them with firm pressure on the gouge. Keep the blade vertical, then rock it right and left to deepen the corners of the eyes, both top and bottom outlines.

Make another trip around the eye sockets trimming just a shaving from around the outside edges of the eyes.

redraw eyes

outline with gouge; press it vertically~ rock left/ right to deepen eye corners

large gouge~ shave from each side of bridge

nostril area-use half of large gouge

use small gouge here

cheek and upper lip~large gouge

With the gouge, trim a series of small chips from either side of the bridge of the nose, giving it the characteristic dip right below the brows. Blend the "bridge" strokes into the eye sockets so that their inner corners are just a little deeper.

Match the corner of the gouge to the outer corner of the nostril, with the rest of the blade heading toward the tip. A firm vertical stroke on ach side will form the nostril area and nose tip. The small gouge will turn each corner.

Use the large gouge to shape the edge of the cheek and upper lip area.

Cherubs

Check the profile diagram to see the curve under the lower lip; shape this with the large gouge. The chin should not stick out father than the base of the nose, so trim the cheeks and jaw line into generous curves that meet in a soft point there. Keep checking the profile on your carving. You can tell from that side view when the features get more realistically aligned.

The mouth detailing is done with the skew knife. Scribe the outline of the separation between the lips first, pressing the knife point firmly into each corner before cutting toward the center. From the center toward the corner, shape each half of the upper lip. You can follow through the cut more easily by working on it turned around.

After righting the project again, shape the lower lip into a generous curve.

In doing the eye detailing, shape them first into a rounded mound by turning the large gouge rounded side up. With the skew knife, cut a tiny sliver from between the lids, where the eye ball would be. This gives the angel a watchful expression.

Model the hair impressionistically with gouge strokes in the direction it grows. Texture it with the large gouge in a series of small scoops across the top and loose waves on the sides. Try pivoting the gouge a little as you cut to make the hair swirl over the ears, which are themselves gouge-size shelves between curls.

Use the chisel with a little mallet tapping to outline the sides of the neck; the gouge will round the bottom. The skew chisel will shape this area.

large gouge shapes the hollow under lower lip

shape jaw and chin

skew knife
1. outline
2. shape ~ best access is like this
3 (turn work upright) round lower lip

turn over large gouge to cut curved eyelid ~ cut matching curve on bottom

skew knife outlines eye opening (remove small chip)

undercut the hair a little bit with the gouge

Undercut means the surface overhangs

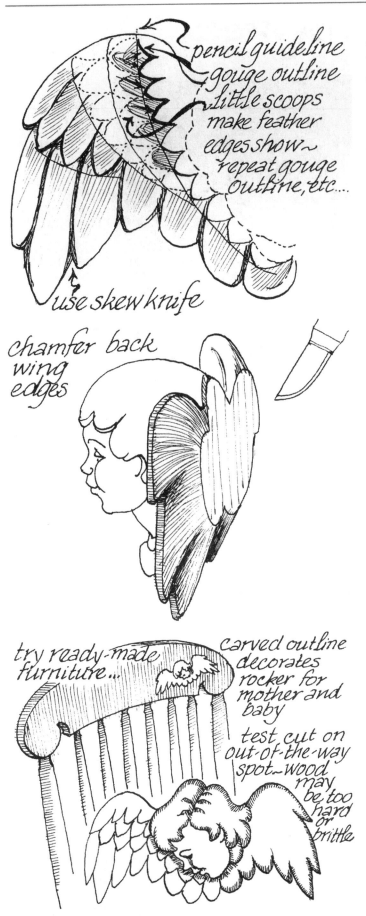

pencil guideline
gouge outline
little scoops
make feather
edges show~
repeat gouge
outline, etc....

use skew knife

chamfer back
wing
edges

try ready-made
furniture...

carved outline
decorates
rocker for
mother and
baby

test cut on
out-of-the-way
spot~wood
may
be too
hard
or
brittle

Ah, the wings! Those feathers are a pattern and texture we can quite enjoy. We kept the hair simple so that the feathers could be extravagant.

The basic wing shape is protectively cupped. The gouge shaping should follow the feathers. Continue the wing curve so that it would seem to go behind the head. Round the leading edges of the curved top of each wing; the big flight feather area can be flatter with a crisp edge.

Feather size is based on the gouge width, with successive rows overlapping like shingles. Unlike shingles, however, your carving will begin on the top row. Use your gouge to mark the height of the first half feather, then pencil that distance down the wing to the angel's neck. Measure off the nest two rows, noting their shorter length.

With the large gouge, firmly outline the top row of feathers, scooping a chip from beneath each that will make the edges show and contours the next row: Repeat the procedure for all of the small feathers.

The fourth row of longer feathers has the same shape tips. On the side of these and the longest feathers, carve a narrow outline trench with the skew knife, to show the separations between them.

When the wings have been feathered, chamfer their back edges with the curved knife. This long slope should taper at the edges, giving the illusion of depth and delicacy without sacrificing strength.

Now you're ready to paint or stain!

The single layer angel can be knife carved into relief, with a good bit of wood removed from outside of the profile and hair, to make them stand out most. You might like to do this carving in just a concise outline, a v-shaped trench made with the angled skew knife cuts, perhaps painting in the detail.

Carousel Horse Heads

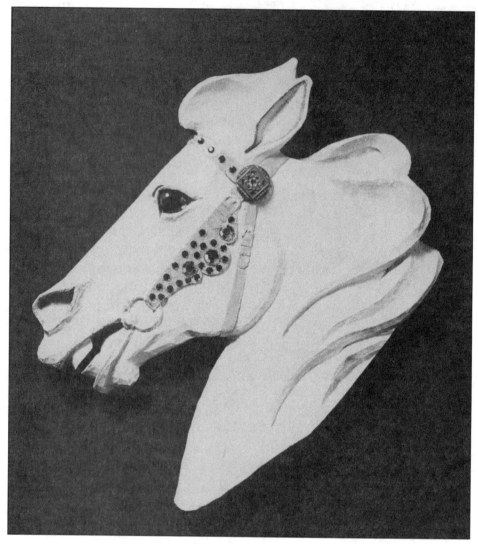

This Carousel-Style Horse in relief has been decorated with jewels and painted. Once carved, you can finish it any way you want—from plain to fancy!

Carousel horse head relief, 10 inches tall x 6¾ inches wide, basswood, painted with artist's acrylics, glazed with fabric paint and glitter, rhinestones, fancy button, has inset glass eye.

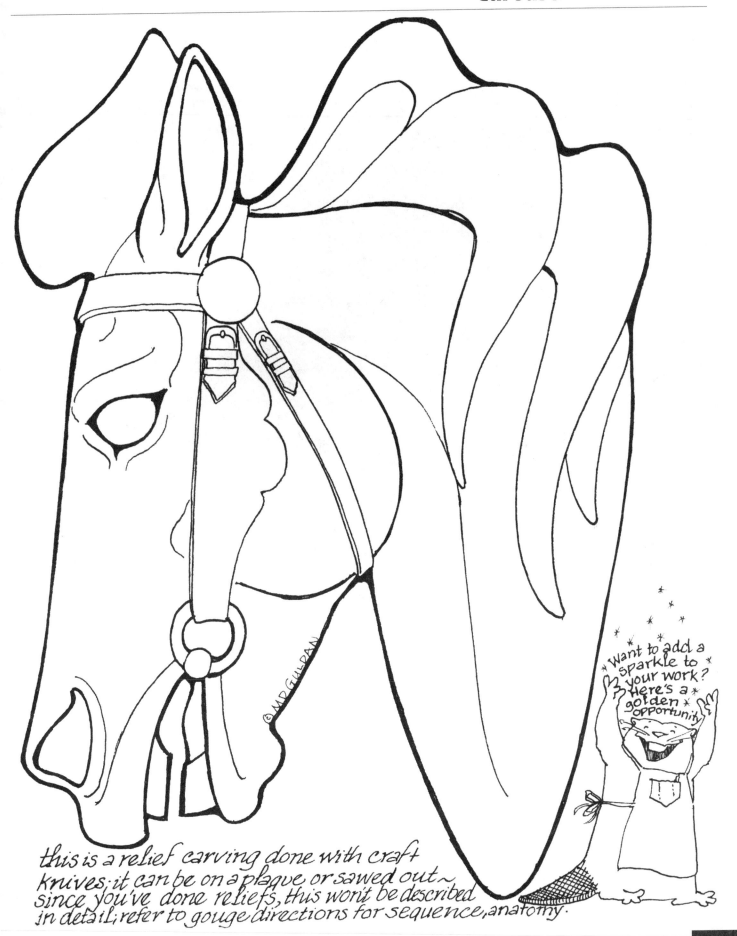

©M.D. GULDAN

Want to add a sparkle to your work? Here's a golden opportunity

this is a relief carving done with craft knives; it can be on a plaque or sawed out ~ since you've done reliefs, this won't be described in detail; refer to gouge directions for sequence, anatomy.

Carousel Horse Head Bookends

These Carousel Horse bookends can be left plain, stained or painted and decorated as above.

Carousel horse head, 6½ inches tall x 5½ inches wide, made two layers of lumber glued together, painted with watercolors, sealed with Minwax Wipe-On Poly, Base is pine, painted with artist's acrylic (cadmium red medium).

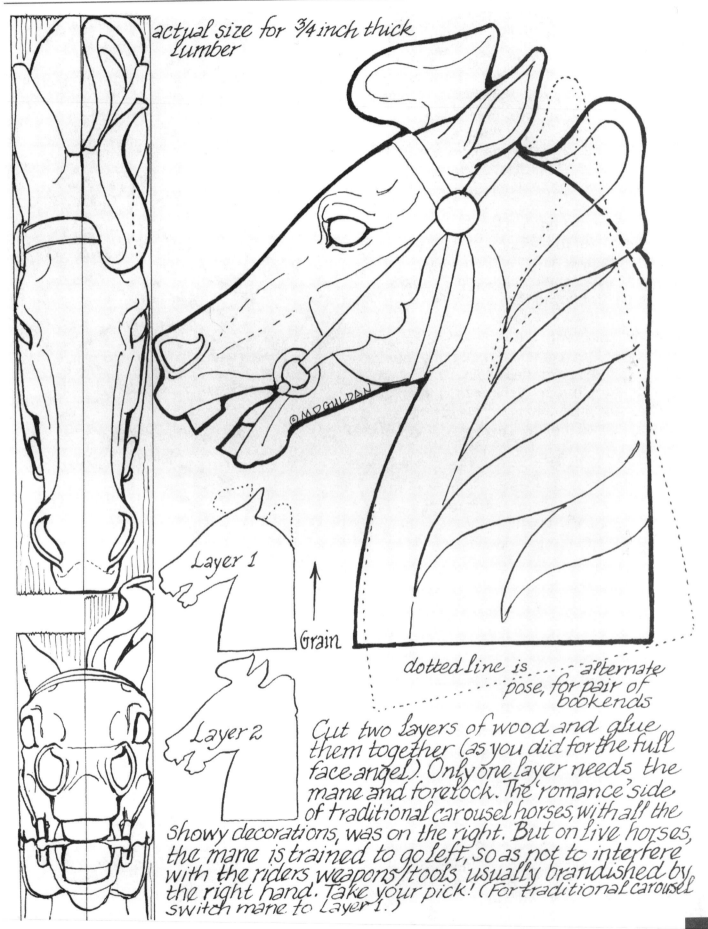

actual size for 3/4 inch thick lumber

Layer 1

Grain

Layer 2

dotted line is .... alternate pose, for pair of bookends

Cut two layers of wood and glue them together (as you did for the full face angel). Only one layer needs the mane and forelock. The 'romance' side of traditional carousel horses, with all the showy decorations, was on the right. But on live horses, the mane is trained to go left, so as not to interfere with the rider's weapons/tools usually brandished by the right hand. Take your pick! (For traditional carousel switch mane to Layer 1.)

©M°GULDAN

Carousel Horse Head Bookends

Carvers who made the old-time wooden carousels knew how to get a lot of horse out of a minimum of material. We're going to do that too. Since your viewers can't resist picking up a dramatic little piece like this, especially when they find out that you made it, we'll keep it carousel sturdy. When you have sawed out and glued together the two layers of wood, clamp them firmly for a good bond. Let the glue dry completely, usually overnight.

Start work with a pencil, marking across the top surface key location to target when you begin roughing out, starting to shape this figure.

With your gouge and mallet, start carving the curve at the top of the neck on the side without the mane, rounding and sloping steeply to the hairline. The curve can continue on the mane to make it seem to blow to the other side.

Use your chisel with the mallet to outline the bottom edge of the ear and jaw, about a quarter inch deep on the top of the jaw line, deepening to a half inch at the throat. With mallet and gouge, shape the hollow beginning just below the ear, continuing behind the jaw, down the length of the neck.

Lower, then round the throat in front of the hollow, and round the muscle in back of it. Slope the back edge of the neck just a little. Continue the curve at the top to just behind the ears.

Check the nostril angle line drawn on top of the blank; with the gouge, carve from the bottom of the nostril area on the side of the face, to exit by that top line.

With the gouge and mallet, start just ahead of the cheek to narrow the face, to the rear of the nostril.

Note on the front view diagram that the nostril and the eye. Round the forehead behind the eye. Angle the ear opening to tilt toward the neck. Curve the forelock as you did the mane.

Narrow the bridge of the nose between the nostril and the ye. Round the forehead behind the eye, Angle the ear opening to tilt toward the neck. Curve the forelock as you did the mane.

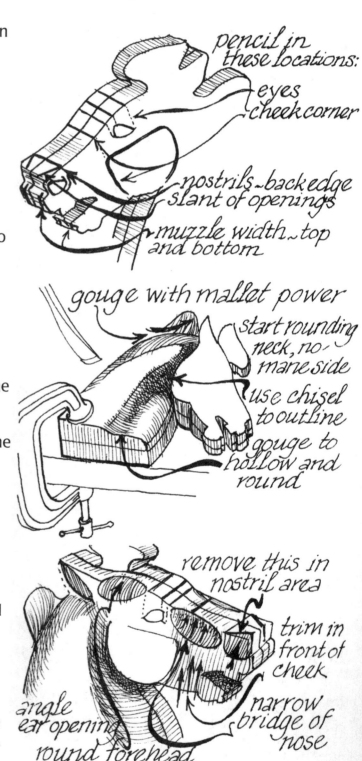

pencil in these locations:
eyes
cheek corner
nostrils ~ back edge
slant of openings
muzzle width ~ top and bottom

gouge with mallet power
start rounding neck, no mane side
use chisel to outline
gouge to hollow and round

remove this in nostril area
trim in front of cheek
narrow bridge of nose
angle ear opening
round forehead

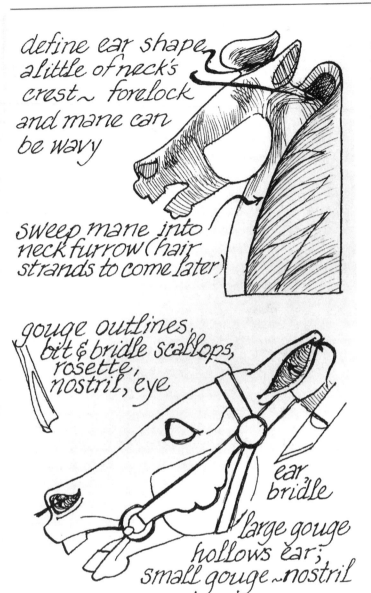

define ear shape, alittle of neck's crest~ forelock and mane can be wavy

sweep mane into neck furrow (hair strands to come later)

gouge outlines, bit & bridle scallops, rosette, nostril, eye

ear bridle

large gouge hollows ear; small gouge~nostril

Loosen the clamp and turn the horse over, securing it again so that you can shape the other side. Follow the same procedures, with the addition of some forelock and mane modeling. When you outline the bottom of the ear with the chisel, do the top also, about a quarter of an inch deep. With the gouge, shape the ear, and then the forelock swirling overhead.

Similarly, outline and shape the crest of the neck, then carve a loop of mane flying up and sweeping down the neck. The rest of the mane follows the shape of the neck in a big curve into that hollow.

Remove the clamp so you can free the horse to make a critical assessment, from all angles. Any additional cuts needed for basic shaping need to be made as soon as the horse is clamped.

Pencil in the bit and bridle, the ear openings, eyes and nostrils. No need to draw the mane yet, the handling will smear it. Remove the clamp so that the features can be drawn on the other side, matching the strap work as needed.

Clamp, then outline the bridle bit's outside edge with the large gouge, push-powered. It will also fit the rosette on the ends of the browband and the scallops on the bridle cheeks. Outline the rest of the bridle with the skew knife.

Use the gouge to outline the eye, pressing firmly. Gouge outline the nostril, bevel deep. Use the skew knife to cut the top outline of the ear opening, tilting the blade to undercut the outline just a little. Cut with the gouge from the lower ear opening line toward the outline cut, making rounded scoops. This need no be deep, or it will make the ear fragile.

With the small gouge, ream out the nostril, angling parallel to the bridge of the nose.

Repeat these steps on the other side. When hollowing the ears and nostril have been done, remove the clamp. The next carving can be done with the knives, on your lap boars, constantly comparing one side of the head to the other.

With the curved knife, shave alongside the bit and bridle, so that they become raised like a tiny shelf. Be conservative, don't cut a trench by accident; the head of a live horse is about two feet long, the straps of a good bridle are an eighth of an inch thick.

Carousel Horse Head Bookends

Outline the edges of the lips, both upper and lower, so that the teeth can be cut to shape underneath. Use the skew knife, round the teeth like a U-turn. Continue the shelf-like lower lip to the bit; notch behind the lower teeth and round the exposed edges of the tongue.

You've rounded eyeballs before; the eyelid is what makes these expressive. Check the horse from head on, where the front of the rounded eyeball should be visible. Trim the edges of the eyelid to widen them in surprise. The eyebrow is a shallow furrow at the front.

Ears are separated the way you did the little dog figure's legs; by cutting a notch between the tips. Gradually cut it wider and deeper until the neck and forelock have been reached. Round the ears, tapering their tips into little points.

Clamp your work carefully, mane side up. Draw swooping strands of mane in pencil, designing them as fanciful as you please.

Use the skew knife to pull long, flowing outline cuts, deep on the root end, shallow over the neck muscle. Your small gouge will clear between the strands; turned on its side, it can reach right up into some small corners. Do remember, though, that there should be the feeling of smooth muscle under the hair, so don't get carried away and carve gullies between the mane strands!

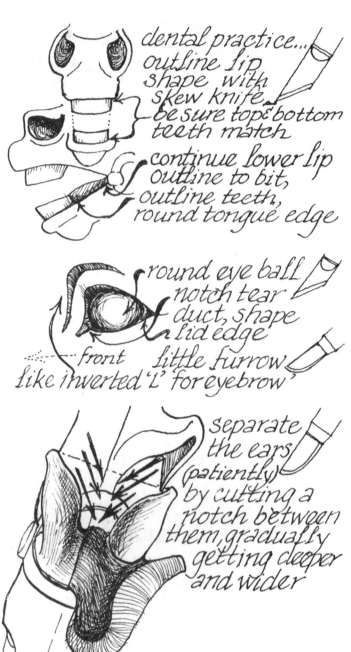

dental practice...
outline lip shape with skew knife.
be sure top & bottom teeth match

continue lower lip outline to bit, outline teeth, round tongue edge

round eye ball
notch tear duct, shape lid edge
front
like inverted 'L' for eyebrow
little furrow,

separate the ears (patiently) by cutting a notch between them, gradually getting deeper and wider

While the work is still clamped, use the small gouge to refine details on the horse's face. Make the nostrils flare by trimming underneath and in front of them. Thin the lips on the sides, make the chin quite peaked. Carefully outline the circle inside the bit ring; scoop a little hollow there. A few light strokes above the cheeks and down the sides of the muzzle suggest muscles. Don't forget to do the corresponding parts on the other side!

When you remove the clamp for the last time, the neck area that it covered can be rounded with your curved knife.

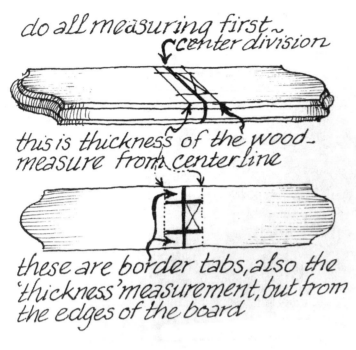

do all measuring first~
center division

this is thickness of the wood~
measure from center line

these are border tabs, also the
'thickness' measurement, but from
the edges of the board

It's easier to paint and decorate this splendid little beast before he's mounted on a base, but let's cover one more construction detail. For the figure to be turned into a bookend, you may have already found a ready-made mounting. I found a wonderful pine nameplate, but it needed to be "folding" in the middle so its shaped edges would follow around corners. Here's the way to do that:

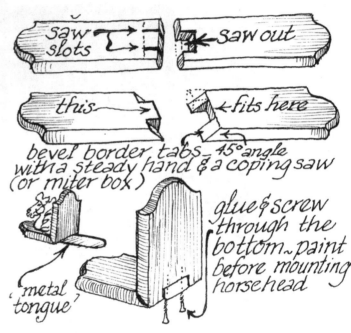

saw slots

saw out

this

fits here

bevel border tabs~ 45° angle
with a steady hand & a coping saw
(or miter box)

'metal tongue'

glue & screw
through the
bottom~ paint
before mounting
horse head

To ensure that the bookend isn't pushed off the shelf by the books, outfitting it with a metal tongue extending from the bottom of its back uses the weight of the books as the anchor. With tin snips I cut the tongue out of a small sheet of aluminum from a model railroad supply. It was screwed to the bottom of the bookend after the horse had been secured with glue and screws.

Wow! What an achievement!

The larger relief horse head is modeled in the same order as the three-dimensional figure, but using craft knives.

An extravagant possibility is the added glass eye. Taxidermist eyes are usually used, but this was a flat backed glass glob used to weight the bottom of a flower vase. Draw a pupil with permanent black felt pen.

Drill lots of close-spaced holes through the eye in front, to guide the hollowing cut from in back. Open the area between the lids, securing the glass from the back of the cavity with thick craft glue or putty. Do not bury the eye; seal the cavity with a cover cut from household baking foil, with a protective piece of cardstock over that. The foil high-lights the eye.

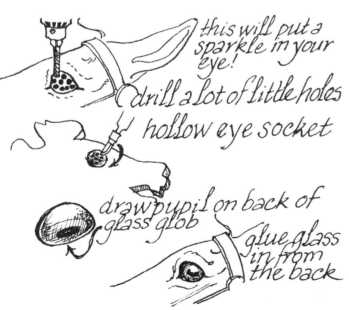

this will put a
sparkle in your
eye!

drill a lot of little holes

hollow eye socket

draw pupil on back of
glass glob

glue glass
in from
the back

Carving Studio Sign

Angled photo shows the profile you are trying to achieve.

Signboard, 13½ inches tall x 9½ inches wide, pine, carved in relief, painted with water colors; embroidery and leaf detail done in permanent fine-point pen, sealed with wipe-on clear satin varnish that has ambered.

Carving Studio Sign

Ready to hang up the relied carvings to enjoy them? Use those little sawtooth bars for hanging pictures. Made of a little strip of metal with notches in the middle and a little "foot" bent into each end, sawtooth bars are only a couple of inches long, so are unobtrusive but effective (and inexpensive as well!). They come in several to the package, complete with small nails to fasten them to a frame. They're available where small household hardware or posters and pictures are sold.

You want to install them a couple of inches from the top in the center of your artwork. To find the center and probable balance point, cut a strip of scrap paper (newspaper, a grocery sack…) a few inches wide and as long as the width of your project. Fold the strip in half and you have the instant center! Put the hanger astride it, teeth down, with a blob of craft glue under each foot. It will help you keep up with the tiny nails when you tap them in with a hammer. Put your project in your lap for this operation to cushion it.

Be warned now, as you're hustling around trying to decide where you'll put your project, if you display your work, you're liable to be barraged by requests (and demands!). Of course, they'll have to catch up with you first, because you're already off, planning your next project!

Now that you're no longer the complete beginner that you once were, back at the beginning of the book, word of your achievement is going to get around. Want to hang out your "shingle?" Here, have a go at mine, and I'll explain some of the "heraldry" so you can do your won, if you want. Despite the fact that the signboard is pine, I like oak leaves and am still as much a collector of acorns as I was when closer to the ground. If you've got a favorite tree, try tracing around some actual leaves and reducing the tracings in a photo copier. Copy the sign pattern (minus the leaves); hold the pattern and you should see them well enough to trace them into your pattern in as many poses as you need.

The tomten is a Scandinavian woodland elf that elderly Finns told Daddy about when he was little, in Minnesota. He told s about tomten when I was little; I looked for him in every hollow tree in the woods and kept just missing him as he'd scamper away, sending nutshells and little bits of bark rattling down the trunk. Tomten were fine craftsmen, and so is Daddy, who goes down to his workshop and makes all kinds of neat things. Now, we can do that too! And you know, there is something elusive and unlikely about taking a blank piece of wood and turning it into an image or figure!

The rabbit is an actual carving in our living room, hewn from the stump of our cedar Christmas tree. My grandfather lavished Brer Rabbit molasses on his toast and talked about the character from long acquaintance. One of that illustrious rabbit's descendants is out in the driveway now, baiting our Airedale on the other side of the fence! What have you got, perhaps in your family folklore that you'd like to immortalize for fun?

Paints, Stains and Hardware

Decoration on those dramatic little horses and other carving projects you've just completed offer great opportunities to explore finishing touches.

Let's consider the horses; the carousel originals were carnival confections sparkling with bright paint, gold leaf and glass "jewels". Sores where fabric and sewing supplies are sold usually have a wide array of acrylic fabric paint to decorate clothing. Some is sparkly or pearlized. These tend to be sort of transparent when brushed on, so glaze them on over a base coat of artist's acrylic paint. Fabric glitter (powered mylar) is meant to be sprinkled onto wet paint or glue; instead, use a dry artist's paint brush to dip it out of the jar and dust it where you want. Have fun!

Fabric stores also carry rhinestones, which perfectly replicate the "jewels" in small scale. Glass rhinestones (sometimes called Austrian or Czech crystal) are preferable because they don't scratch or get dull and aren't affected by paint or glue solvents. These can be glued on and painted over, then wiped clean afterward. Use a wooden toothpick to wipe off their edges. Fancy buttons and costume jewelry, especially earrings, make splendid bridle decorations.

For the look of "antique factory paint" on your horse, try watercolors protected by varnish. A boxed set of watercolors in little pans, to be moistened with water as needed, works well, because no details get buried by the paint and the wood grain still shows. If you plan to varnish, don't use blue or purple paint; they turn funny colors as the varnish ages and yellows. Manufacturers call the "ambering." If you use a wipe-on type of varnish or resin (Minwax Wipe-On Poly or Watco Danish Oil Finish are two) for a very handsome no-shine satin finish, it will amber quite a lot. This is a valuable characteristic, however, because it mellows your carving to heirloom quality in just a few years!

Commercially made stains to finish wood are widely available; if you've worked with wood before, you probably have your favorites. Their very uniform color may not show off your carvings as well as one you mix yourself. Pick out tubes of artist's oil paint colors that you really like. Most brands include a sample band of color on the label. Burnt umber is a warm, friendly brown that works well in any intensity; Paynes gray is a weathered wood to smoky dark color and very versatile.

Fold a little shallow tray out of alum-inum baking foil for a disposable palette. Squeeze out an inch or two of oil paint near one corner. Pour a little puddle of varnish, or wipe-on varnish (any clear satin finish that cleans up with turpentine), and with a brush, mix a little paint and a little varnish to inten-sity that you like. Test this on the back or bottom of your piece; it will dry a little lighter. Paint it on, mixing more as needed.

While you wouldn't want a distracting stripe, color with slight variations enhances your carving. Highlights with more varnish, less color, or shadows with more color make the most of the shaping that you did. If the color is too light when it dries, glaze on another coat.

Artist's acrylic paints, which are water-soluble until dry, are waterproof after drying, tough and durable, easy to mix and fairly fast drying. They do not need to be sealed afterward the way watercolors require, though they are as easy to use. Generally, "what you see is what you get", and their color changes little when dry.

Sources

There are many good sources both local stores and mail-order for tool and wood. Here are a few that I am familiar with. The best guide to sources for woodcarvers is the Spring Suppliers issue of Chip Chats magazine. Please see the following pages for information on this magazine from the National Wood Carvers Association. Your local supplier is a treasure trove of information on classes, clubs, etc.

CraftWoods
2101 Greenspring Drive
Timonium, MD 21093
(410) 561-9444
(410) 560-0760 FAX
Carving tools, wood, paint, tools, decoy carving supplies

Craftsman Wood Service Co.
1735 W. Cortland Ct.
Addison, IL 60101
800-543-9367
(708) 629-8292 FAX
Basswood lumber by the square foot, carving tools, woodworking supplies

Woodcraft
210 Wood County Industrial Park
PO Box 1686
Parkersburg, WV 26102-1686
800-225-1153
(304) 428-8271 FAX
Carving tools, mallets, woodworking finishes and supplies

Klockit
PO Box 636
Lake Geneva, WI 53147-0636
800-556-2548
(414) 248-9899 FAX
Clock movements, numerals, supplies, carving tools

Woodcarver's Guide to Sharpening, Tools and Setting Up Shop (Best of WCI)
ISBN: 978-1-56523-475-8 **$19.95**

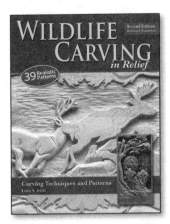

Wildlife Carving in Relief
ISBN: 978-1-56523-448-2 **$24.95**

Whittling Little Folk
ISBN: 978-1-56523-518-2 **$16.95**

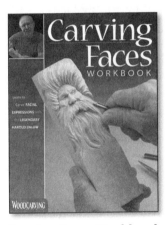

Carving Faces Workbook
ISBN: 978-1-56523-585-4 **$19.95**

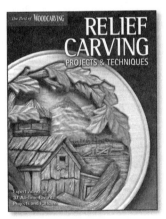

Relief Carving Projects & Techniques (Best of WCI)
ISBN: 978-1-56523-558-8 **$19.95**

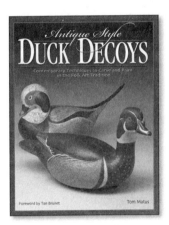

Antique-Style Duck Decoys
ISBN: 978-1-56523-298-3 **$19.95**

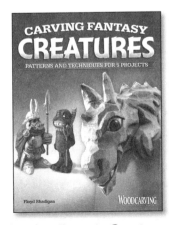

Carving Fantasy Creatures
ISBN: 978-1-56523-609-7 **$12.99**

Big Book of Whittle Fun
ISBN: 978-1-56523-520-5 **$12.95**

Carving Spoons - 2nd Edition
ISBN: 978-1-56523-227-3 **$14.95**

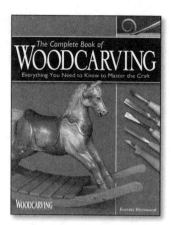
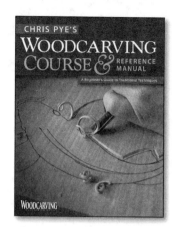
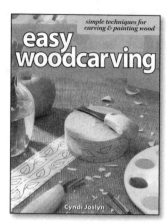
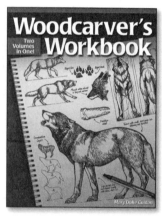